BONFIRES

BONFIRES

CHRIS BANKS

For Janet,
I hope you!
enjoy the poems!
Chris Banks
Toronto, 2003

A Junction Book

NIGHTWOOD EDITIONS

ROBERTS CREEK, BC

2003

Nightwood Editions
R.R. #22, 3692 Beach Ave.
Roberts Creek, BC
V0N 2W2, Canada

We gratefully acknowledge the support of the Canada Council for the Arts and the British Columbia Arts Council for our publishing program.

NATIONAL LIBRARY OF CANADA CATALOGUING IN PUBLICATION

Banks, Christopher, 1970–
        Bonfires / Chris Banks.

Poems.
"A Junction Book".
ISBN 0-88971-196-8

        I. Title.

PS8553.A564B66 2003   C811'.6   C2003-905283-4

For my parents

Contents

IN THE DIRECTION OF LITTLE TOWNS

If you drive down the fourth line, you see meadow
        and field, creek and riverbed—
swathed in sunlight—and perhaps cattle, heads slung
        low or else lying down
if there is going to be rain. A few intersections point
        in the direction of little towns
you knew and grew up in, while others are signless,
        and lead further away from

the familiar, expected places toward names on maps
        that may or may not still exist.
A murder of crows rises like buckshot from rows
        of green corn. Your car speeds past
a red farmhouse with a white sign on its lawn
        announcing *Christ Died*
for the Ungodly. Everything disassembles itself
        into some new clarity here,

like that chain-link fence you passed which leads
        through bushland to a waterfall
and broken beer bottles, or that old stone farm
        where two boys, a decade ago, climbed up a silo
and fell through fathoms of grain, panic filling their mouths
        before calm overtook them, or those
high bluffs you passed two miles back, where
        you once sat with your first love

watching two hawks circle each other,
     some invisible blade held firmly between their talons,
threshing the air, caught up in a rhythm
     shared with dark green hills and
wide skies, a rhythm both your lover and you felt,
     were pulled into, for hours her body
cradling your own that long afternoon. While now
     a little further down the road

your car motors past other details: the cracked
     stubble of a fallow field,
a river's black chattering teeth, a bird's splintering trill—
     all leading you back to where
you have always been, as if going anywhere
     is to leave something behind,
scattered like pollen or apple blossoms,
     on the waft of summer air.

I

THE COUNTRY OF OUR EXILE

If this were the country of our exile.
If this were home.

Rhea Tregebov

LONGING

You live a year without a woman leaving her impression softly
outlined, etched into the mess of sheets, dimpled on the right
side of the bed, and you think *Good, I am getting somewhere....*

But each day becomes harder, more strenuous, and it takes
all of your spirit to fight off the desire shuttered in your eyes,
the longing you keep tamped down like a hurricane inside

a child's locket, or stopped up within the cask of the heart.
So much so, you begin to avoid public places that seem
to worsen the condition, like bars or restaurants, but then

disaster strikes in the middle of a checkout, or on a bus
when a woman flashes you a smile, and you flee in terror
to the back of the line, or by getting off at the next corner.

Your outstretched hands still proffering pencil and paper
to the open air, while you congratulate yourself for not
asking for her number, for a close call averted. But later

at home, in the hours of lengthening dusk, you can feel
its presence growing, the dull ache, a recomposing of pain.
What it is trying to say, and how it is probably right.

ARGUMENTS

for Cass

Moonlight clasps the floorboards,
the walls resonant
with sounds of our shared lungs
moving a cavern of air.

The argument forgotten
at the dinner table
like leftovers
for tomorrow's breakfast.

In four months time,
there will be one final argument,
but for now

there is simply our breathing,
the slough of moonlight,
and the slow erasure of self
insulating us from whatever it is
we cannot overcome.

Stumbling Home

Stumbling home, pockets emptied of bills
      donated to a local bar,
I'm feeling drunk and rudderless. No one else out walking
      at this late hour, only
the electric hum of street lights, insects,
      passing black cars—
unseen occupants driving toward destiny
      or something less fickle,
tenderness or misery, whatever awaits us
      at daybreak.

My voice tries to sing, but betrays me an instant later.
      My unforgiving legs
push me up and down these sidewalks
      like embarrassed parents.

There are stars in the sky, perfect enigmas of indifference,
      and litter on the streets.
If I close my eyes, I can hear my own blood beating
      its fugue of soft hammers—

still see a nacreous moon shining
      over the condominiums.

THIRTY-ONE

This morning I woke to find the coffee tin empty,
three unpaid bills in the mailbox, a six-pack of beer,
well-dry, in the kitchen sink, my nephew's baby photos
stuck to a fridge magnet and suddenly I am thirty-one,
only believing what I can touch or see. A dull breeze
clatters into the room as if to say, *Life is absence
no matter how you try to fill it.* Somewhere in India,
our lives are written down for us on palm leaves.
So why go on collecting the gas bills and the tax receipts?
The stamps and the coupons? Our lives are elsewhere
and have been for centuries. In my backyard, birds
sing in my cherry tree like a choir of exiles.

FORM LETTERS

Walking out of my house in early summer,
heat lisps sweat from my skin. It is

mid-morning. Leaves hang sigil-like
from iron branches. What import is written there,

we have forgotten to read. Traffic sounds,
commuters rushing off to work or private attendances,

gull us to believe life is panic. Model homes
stand incommunicado across the street.

They cast a pall upon the chemical-green lawns.
My postman arrives with his bag of correspondences

and hands me six white letters. I hand him a poem.
It is done. We turn in opposite directions.

He looks down and his eyes fill with poetry.
I read my mail: *Miracles do happen, make your dreams*

come true, free yourself today, celebrate summer,
claim your prize, be happy.

Domestic Wages

Five dead snails lie in the saucer of beer I filled last night from
the bottoms of four cans of Kilkenny, dregs my dog didn't want,

and left out near the strawberry patch where they'd been wreaking
havoc with this year's crop—but now dead, sent into the darkness

their shells grew from, and the sun is high in the afternoon skies,
making it difficult to believe in notions of infinity, something beyond

my own limited understanding of the world, its virtues and vices,
where killing snails in one's garden seems a great injustice to

a God who is neither in the world, nor makes himself known to it,
so that we must invent other rituals: rising each morning to face

the drive to work, the queue at the coffee shop, office parties,
then home again to empty houses, and memories of ex-lovers

falling into the arms of new loves, things we've struggled, worked
our whole lives for—and could rightly call domestic wages,

for we earn them through our luck and our labour, all of time
pushing through us, and beyond us, making it harder each day

to separate the divine from the trivial—or what meaning might
be found in a few snails lying dead in a pool of amber beer.

The dog stoops in a corner of the yard.
A toad sits under a tree, its skin bronzed
by rain. Baloo wags his tail, crouches, barks
twice. The toad, unresponsive, blinks
cold, amphibian eyes, keeping silent
its own private truth. Incautiously, Baloo cusps
the little creature like old leather, a lost shoe
or a baseball mitt, something to be mulled over
at one's leisure. I watch his mouth rasping
over the toad's skin, the small, benign tumors
gathered to taste, the conflicting scents of flowers,
crabgrass, loam. A high whimper. His whole body
surrenders a shudder. His look, so urgent,
tells the story all dogs come to learn.
Baloo drops the sagging pouch of bones
and retreats a little diminished across the lawn,
what remains of the toad's mystery
threading his jowls, the untrimmed grass
murmuring beneath his treading feet.

BACKYARD

The air we remember
is the last breath taken
on a warm June night,
a light breeze crushing rabbit paths
in the rivering grass
and the hemorrhage of stars
high above the trees

leaves us no words, only white,
unblinking mysteries to light
the paths we tread
like the billions of cells
lighting up the galaxy
within our heads.

So we live, seeing
and mis-seeing,
watching the dog piss
in the backyard, his nose
abuzz like a switch
unable to turn off
the darkness,

before running back
to brush up against us,

against the fear
our bodies feel but cannot contain—
a formlessness that says
we are adrift under the only sky
we will ever know.

ALLERGIES

The white coma of a sneeze
takes you mid-yawn,
        like an early August epiphany;
histamine slow burning nerves,
        drowning you in the deep end of sense.

Your throat grows scales. The greenness
of your lawn plays guerilla warfare
        with plush, clogged sinuses.
Pollens infiltrate the body, the bloodstream,
        wrack you in sogged sneezes—

until finally, in September, a lethal frost
chernobyls the last of the sagebrush, the ragweed,
        ending your affliction; roots sinking
deeper into the earth, into a post-mortem darkness
        awaiting resurrection.

SIGNS OF LEAVING

You feel it, in September,
when little birds
in piffling speech,
start to lip-sync
time-worn melodies
of ample uselessness
while trees sit
like Buddhists on hills

whisper *om*
after a pale wind
walks through
stripping branches
to an essential
bareness beneath.

Everywhere there
are signs of leaving:
Canada geese
are flying south,

young couples
wake up all over town
no longer in love

and brown trout
are running up river
like bayonets
stabbing against
the stream.

Subtle signatures
awakening in us
that animal need to
leave it all behind—

and begin again.

DECEMBER

It is December and no birds sing.
Empty nests hang like ornaments in the trees.
My dog moves along the winding path,
stopping occasionally to test his nose
on a naked branch, and when I call to him,
fearing he has strayed too far,
I watch the name I gave him years ago
sing through his bones and for a moment
he hesitates, the animal in him
wanting to go further into these woods
where names, words, won't reach.

Wintering Place

The sky is dawning; a new lavender
where birds, caught in lariats of wind,
range from the clouds' upper battlements

to stipple early morning fields
with their mortal presence. Who I am
or who you claim to be scarcely matters;

only the smell of ozone settling
over our clothes, the blood scribing praise
through our hearts. And these birds

who need to find a wintering place:
dark wings beating against the wet and damp,
lifting into the absence of the earth.

II

Bonfires on the Road to Nowhere

We feel it ourselves, a bright uncertainty of what's to come.

Charles Wright

For a day each landowner lit great bonfires and then walked, torch in hand, as far as he could advance from dawn to dusk. The lands he symbolically burned would be those he could hold in title.

Stephen J. Pyne, *Fire: A Brief History*

Bonfires on the Road to Nowhere

Above the town of Iqaluit,
a narrow road locals call
The Road to Nowhere skirts
through the land's stone margins,

a place in evenings where
teenagers gather to talk and smoke,
crowding around fires, bodies
seeking heat of other bodies,

easy conversation making everyone
feel somnolent and restful, expansive,
in this ocean of miles and seeing,
light carouselling like a mirage,

The Road to Nowhere going through the land
and through them, like a beginning
without end, the dust of each breath
kissing the small feet of each stone.

Sioux Lookout, Hwy. 9

Moon-feathered pines
fête the highway.
My brother and I

packed in the back
of a rusted K-car,
north of Superior—

scragged hills,
silver-shirred lakes,
the long drive

across midnight
taking longer than
we wished to go—

our parents silent,
distant like
galaxies expanding

in opposite directions.
Look out your window
my mother warns—

aurora borealis,
its green turbulence,
back-lit by stars

dopplering the sky
while we stare
wordlessly at its

uncanny incandescence—
our car moving
stealthily beneath:

a phantom aircraft
ghosting on NORAD's
early warning system.

Far North

This night walk the pebbled road to the bay.
Watch as you pass men and women leaving the local bar.
Their bodies mugged by wind. Totems carved human.
Remember how earlier you lay awake for hours
under arctic skies banked with granite light

listening to the injured cries of the pack,
the hunting and the killing in the luminous streets;
how the bright voices of young children
came to your window long past midnight
to celebrate the simple magic of play.

The sky you walk under is no one's sovereignty.
The land a palace of stones. Night is
the colour of dawn, the colour of the ocean
dreaming at the feet of white hills. Ice floes
drift across the bay like cap-sized ships.

Tomorrow, only this light will exist.

PANMUNJOM, DMZ

A caterpillar clings to a rail of grass,
its small claim to life its poignancy.
A troop of North Korean soldiers
stand motionless on the horizon
trying to gauge the human distance
these hills make you feel. In the wind
music is founded, five blackbirds sing
in the heart of a tree. History is lost
amongst the stones and the pebbles.
Land mines flower along dark shores
underground: black petals open.
They listen for all sides to approach.

BOOK OF CHANGES

i. Cheju-do

Women divers bob in the surf
like white buoys,
vanish down rungs of green water
to catch sea creatures
asleep in their shells.

Their mothers gather on shore
sell squid, anemone, octopus,
from plastic pails. Watermarked faces
chiselled by sea and sun.

Already, I miss this island—
the mountain's green complexion,
its ocean full of women.

ii. Beijing

Where are the missing persons
among the families, tourists
snapping pictures
under Mao's gaze.

Where are the missing voices?

If it wasn't for the morning
rain, the square filling
with people, boy soldiers in green,
or hawkers of postcards,

I'd swear I could hear
the speeches, tanks rolling in—

what is unspoken.

iii. *Prague*

Within the smallest movements of our lives
an order to what is—little mercies.
Two children catching frogs in a drainage ditch,
a lost mitten in the schoolyard, and these
old men sitting beside a stream
in a country not my own
looking for the river princes they once were.

iv. *Naxos*

Night's music in the streets
is the sea's song, a half mile off,
breaking against rocks.

I have been broken by passions
great as the sea, carried
the sound of waves, dark waters,
like a song within me.

But now, in the presence
of the sea's voice, its injuries,
I am left to ask,

am I broken or am I intact?

v. Seoul

How small is the night,
the moon's white flare,
the body going out
into forgetfulness.
And out of its dark room
come the lost stories
we know as dreams,
beautiful and inscrutable
as the energy of stars;
the weight of light
passing through.

Long Road to China

I'm driving from the airport in Beijing
through downtown streets made ashen
by a million coal fires burning,

and I'm looking for a reason
as to why I've chosen this route:
this taxi with its tinted windows,

its poor excuse for a cabbie
who keeps trying conversation
asking if I'm American.

I politely say "No" and he smiles,
lighting a Marlboro cigarette,
a robber baron who knows

he is making sixty dollars
on a twelve-dollar fare, and
there will be no protestations

from the last tourist to learn
you should never leave your pack
in the trunk of a car in a country

where you are neither Chinese
nor Communist. Despite this,
I smile at my pirate chauffeur,

watch the black rain of bicycles
pedalling the narrow streets of Beijing,
knowing I chose with purpose

to drive off into a mystery,
beyond restraint or nagging doubt,
wanting only to arrive.

OUR LADY OF THE CORNFIELDS

They mark the sadness and grief of being loved
loved so intensely it is like a flame

Al Purdy

Yesterday, she revealed herself to me
on the edge of the Trans-Canada,
amid the cornfields and wood-gutted barns:

a statue of the Virgin, arms wide open,
blessing the tonnage of passing cars
en route from Cornwall to Quebec City.

Our Lady of the Cornfields, I whispered,
scanning her plastered face.
Someone's crushing faith worn

like an invisible garment around her.
And for a moment I felt
something akin to faith rise

warmly in my chest, corralled deeply
within—and then nothing—
but highway and her behind me

standing in a basilica of corn, my car just
another in a long line of witnesses
edging towards other stations.

WHEN ALREADY YOU HAVE COME SO FAR

Outside the city limits at night, the road becomes
        one long parade of nothingness
on the drive home from Toronto. There is the scrum
        of headlights in other lanes,

the moon windowed high above, racing the 401,
        and the unseen cities you pass
without seeing where the exit signs actually take you.
        Late-night radio signals

move invisibly through the car, filling the speakers,
        reminding you of long distances
travelled over a lifetime, each dialled FM station
        lulling you back

to a high school or a university, or a childhood
        filled with Neil Diamond songs
at a cottage no longer your own. Late-night hosts
        talk crassly, so you turn off

the radio and your thoughts tune to other reverberations—
        the wheels' turning,
the mind's turning, the night's turning—and in between,
        tiny rivulets of silence

underpinning every moment, pulling you in and out
        of yourself, as your car passes
road signs telling you how far you've come—
        how far there is still to go.

III

WAS THIS WHAT YOU CAME FOR?

Explorer, you tell yourself this is not what you came for
although it is good here, and green;

Gwendolyn MacEwen

HIDING UNDER THE COTTAGE PORCH

Sunlight clad in bright hues of summer.
I am hiding under the cottage porch.
My grandfather is singing my name.

My name is sinking in a corner of the bay.
The green air transmits its cloudless frequency.
A fish jumps. Relatives stampede

the yard, circle round, do not find me:
I am not playing among the hummingbirds;
the cowled heads of my grandmother's flowers.

Waves rasp dangerously against the shoreline.
My uncle dives off the dock, his body jackknifes,
splitting the blue vault of the lake.

My grandfather is singing my name.
My name is gathering. I hear it calling:
I'm here. I'm here. I'm here.

THE OLD POND

for my brother

Two small boys sit at the pond's edge,
dipping cool hands into water,
sun blazing, catching crayfish, frogs,
making a competition of summer.
Each day they get better, more skilled,
at becoming hunters of the pond's green secrets,
air teasing its shorn surface, small hands
disappearing momentarily below the waterline,
coming up with pollywogs like black commas
cupped in fists. Weeks moving into weeks,
lives moving into other lives. Still the boys
are too young to see or know what is emerging
from the present moment. They see only
an old pond, lichenous rocks, translucent frog eggs,
a summer's worth of green creatures to catch
and hold aloft like cereal box prizes, gifts
of a childhood in passing, the two boys
struggling to not let them slip free.

My Brother's Keeper

Don't hurt me, you say,
your voice coming from
inside the locked truck

while I circle smiling on
the hottest day of August
with parents at work and

childhood rules for settling
scores on both our minds.
The bruise, the tattoo of

a fist pools green-black
under my left eye, after
your less-than-successful

hit-and-run, and now
my anger is something
you will not outlast, so

you start to cry behind
the truck's windshield
as I stare through it

threatening to scatter
your teeth like grass seed
across the wide yard.

My Father Wanted to Be a Cowboy

1.

My father wanted to be a cowboy
so spent childhood afternoons
out of the house, at the movies,
not knowing what it was
about men in unwashed mackinaws
riding the earth's blue curve
that he admired, only knowing
he loved how they wandered
old before the dawn. The sun
rising so orange in the hills
it makes a man forget
the sad creature he resembles
riding west upon a horse.
A stranger with a gun.

2.

My father wanted to be a cowboy
so left home at eighteen. Imagine him
riding off into the sunset on his trusty bicycle,
away from his parents, the half-drunk bottles,
the leather belt hanging on the kitchen wall.
He delivered groceries for two years
before meeting my mother, waiting 'til
they had exchanged names and pleasantries
before he declared "I wanna be a cowboy.
Let's get hitched." She just laughed.

3.

My father made his living as a policeman.
He won occasional awards for sharpshooting,
public merit. Sometimes his parents would call
wanting money for the hydro, the gas bill,
back payments on the house, whatever, but
my father was always too quick on the draw
to be taken so unawares. He'd wait patiently
on the other end of the line, throat constricted,
brown, rawhide eyes reddening, mouth
tight as he breathed ". . . I just can't,"
the surface of his voice flowing like slow water.
It's true what they say about a cowboy's life
being like a poor hand of solitaire.

4.

The cowboy's life was hard on my mother,
the constant moving, the loss of friends.
Her heart, my heart, scored with saddle sores.
We never got used to the ambushes,
the sudden gunfights with shadowy riders
on pale horses. They who always found us,
better than any Pinkerton,
when our backs were turned.

5.

Sometimes I see my father
staring off into far green hills,
his mind a trail leading back
to blue sky country, whatever memories
he keeps pastured there, his body,
rough-hewn, cast in the glow
of some boyhood dream: *If only
I had a horse, if only I could sing. . . .*
There, angels play pedal-steel guitar
as he kicks up his heels, rides
out of town, the whole earth aglow
from the sparks of his silver spurs
striking the dying, amber sun.

Halloween

It was the phone call's urgency,
my mother running outside with her nurse's bag
under one arm, that tore the day loose
from the vagaries of childhood.

Later I found out when Dad got home
the old drunk who lived two blocks over
swung his car into a ditch, walked home,
took the business end of a rifle, stuck it
beneath his chin, and pulled the trigger.

It was like he was wearing a Halloween mask,
my father said when the man answered the door,
face half-blown off, the wood-grained rifle,
lying quiet as a corpse on the floor.

Years later, in university, a friend of mine
suffering from nightmares, depression,
asked *What does it mean when you want to die*
and still you go on living? I told her I imagine
a man standing at a door, with no nose

or lower jaw, flesh of tongue hanging limp, a snail
without a shell, my parents keeping him alive
until the ambulance could arrive. His eyes
saying everything his mouth could not.

Through the Walls

Sometimes, out of the darkness,
a voice rises, bodiless, full of reprises
and jettisoned loves, garotting

what is left of its source. Knowing
it is my mother, moist-eyed and
pain-deep, crying into her phone,

it strikes me what separates
our lives at this moment is more
than 2x4's, plaster and drywall—

it is the dark spillways of the past
and its unmentionables—that voice
sequestered inside a sadness

I recognize and at times feel also,
when later I hear her drop the phone
to cry against my bedroom walls.

Was This What You Came For?

Remember stealing out from your parents' house
at thirteen, to meet girls, their freckled breasts
hidden under Quiet Riot t-shirts, the musk

of midnight vespering in the summer pines,
blood tindering its one basso note in your veins.
What was it about those childhood games

in the covert darkness—boys against girls,
which sent surges of fear and a new presence,
hormones shunting through the brain's static,

each time you pulled one of them giggling down
into the wet fields of the ballpark?
Each kiss became an encounter you later

tried to reassemble from memory
on the way home, wondering what it was
you wanted, what it was you came for,

your shirt smelling of wet grass,
skinny girls like spiced apples, their flesh so close—
that scent clinging to everything.

Magnetic Hill

We ditched our afternoon classes
on the first day of spring, giddy
with the breeze we felt in the air,
its renegade scent, its fullness: an earthy
cologne of apples and pig shit kicked up
by the solitary combines working in
the freshly sweetened fields. We went
to find the magnetic hill somewhere
between Creemore and Mansfield,
information passed between friends,
then giggled as someone's green Impala
lurched up its soft sloping rise under
no horsepower save that of the infinite —
or at least, something as inexplicable
to teenagers who knew little about physics
or the dark machinery of the earth,
what forces, for good or for bad, govern us all
and are so powerful, so invisible
they could well up through a gravel road,
push a car the length of a small room,
before retreating, subsiding into
a cold cellar of iron and nickel,
quartz and copper, lying in low yields
under nestled green fields, a terrestrial

magic abating, like a reverse tremor,
an earthquake gone back into the quiet,
after some sign had been granted.
Later, I discovered something of that
experience, deep and subterranean,
stayed within me through the years
so I recognized its invisible tug-o-war,
the pull of a world larger than myself
whenever situations would arise
that could not be explained by reason,
or controlled by circumstance, or
wished away by tears, and in those
moments of awe, or grief, when my life
became something so heavy, I had
the sudden notion to fall upon my knees
from the weight of it all; it was
that restless energy, the earth's sudden
insistence that kept pulling me
forward through this life,
whether I wanted it to or not.

There is a young man, obviously drunk,
standing in the middle of an intersection
outside of a club on a Friday night. Arms
outstretched, he points towards the streaking cars
rushing up to greet him. Their headlights,
little aureoles, scald the night-air white,
as they move closer to the sullen young man
who decides to sit in the middle of the street
atop his jean jacket, like that famous picture
of the Buddhist monk on fire. What he is
protesting, his fist raised in a gesture
raw, emblematic, I do not know.

What I do know is I cannot look away.
Cars brake, and hands move onto horns
as he yells obscenities. I imagine
an argument back in the bar, or else
a simple bout of jealousy, the sort of distress
a boy who finds himself in a man's body
can only quash through summoning rage.

His friends call for him to get up, to come back
across the road, and then I see her—a young girl
by their side choking back violent sobs. But already,
I can see he is gone from them. His eyes contain
that stubborn look that says he has crossed
over in his mind to a place beyond tenderness
or reasoning, beyond fear or love. There is now
only the alcohol moving like a trade wind
through his brain, and the subsequent
brownout of his thoughts, that coma,
and perhaps, in the end, this is all he wants,
not to feel, not to feel anything, except the rage
which he mistakes for a kind of freedom:
his sitting in the streets like a man on fire,
while car horns blare, and people shout, his anger
like a living flame, rising up to meet them.

GRAVEYARD

It seems strange looking back
at high school, when we
would ride out to Creemore

in the July heat, a case of Export
smuggled out of someone's garage
into a friend's trunk, rolling across

the iron bridge, the Mad River
dusted with mayflies, passing into
the graveyard, high on the hill.

Sometimes we brought girls,
other times just drank beer,
celebrated our youth, who we were

in those moments, often
stripping naked, clowning around,
but never disturbing the dead

who really didn't care much,
and why a graveyard, or that
graveyard, I can't remember

except to say it was beautiful
in the July heat, that we were
young men, who drank beer,

who collected their empties
and like the dead, took no
notice of our lives passing.

IV

What's Left to Wonder About

*…Since nothing is so secret or hidden that it cannot be revealed,
everything depends on the those things that manifest the hidden…*

Paracelsus

Cinéma Vérité

You sit night after night, at a table or a desk,
windows thick with stars, trying to give form
to something you feel is missing in your life,

but isn't missing, just misplaced, like a movie
where the guy everyone thought was dead
really isn't, and comes back in the big finale.

This is the Hollywood ending, not your own,
not even midstream through your thirties
where hope plays the part of the millionaire recluse,

and despair that of the angry kid who takes joy
in keying the shiny red hood of your heart,
leaving only your doubts to follow you home

to shoot a documentary called *The Off Hours*,
about your life or lack of it. And when you see it
playing in your neighbourhood, you take it in,

making comments like: *Oh, I don't talk like that,*
until realizing that sad pretender, that poor rube
talking up on the screen, he's all you have left.

THE HUNGER STRIKER

He sat in the cold end of many weeks.
His mind shouldering starvation's dead weight.
In the hard days to follow, he came to view
the body as a kind of sumptuous fruit.
A golden food the stomach consumed.
He came to see God in the face of this.
To know himself was all he had meant
to learn from the spirit. The end of himself
was all he had meant to teach the flesh.
He thought of Gandhi fasting for workers' rights
at the textile mills at Ahmedabad, and of St. Patrick
on Crochan Aigh for forty days without food,
tormented by demons in the form of blackbirds.
When guards found him the next morning
gone so deeply into that place where
hunger could no longer reach him,
they knew he had found his home.

What the Dead Won't Let Go

What the dead
won't let go
is the thought

we continue
placidly on
without them;

that some debt
is owed
for settling

into the riffs
of our lives, not
resurrecting

them from
memories, or thoughts;
and instead

choosing to forget
what they
came to know

too late in life:
that the death
of a loved one

is an emptiness
that will one day
contain us, too.

Gardeners in Paradise

Leaves turn colour every day of the year
in Heaven, yet never fall from their boughs.
And all gardeners find employment

in Paradise, although no one trims
so much as a twig or a branch, knowing
Eternity roots itself in perfection.

Oh, they'd chop off their green thumbs
if they thought it would do any good,
but everything here just grows back,

more vital and effusive. Evergreen.
Such proud men in the heart of creation
crying into useless hands. I tell you,

gardeners are the loneliest creatures
in Paradise. Everything grows tall
and alien and beautiful in spite of them.

Whispering Angels

for Paul

I'm tired of you winged bastards
comin' round here
in the most godless hours of night

to roust upon my headboard, scattering
feathers like frosted glass across
the bedspread, whispering poems like postcards
sent from Heaven's bordertowns.

Save your prayers, I've heard 'em all.
I'll come praise you dutifully in my own time.
Find you nestled in stone puttos,
or green arbours,

Or behind the faces of
street people in my neighbourhood.

Until then, go bother Vermeersch for a while.
He works late anyways.

i. *The Mirror-Maker*

The mirror-maker arrives home drunk and late,
spirits lifted higher than a full moon over
the churches of Murano. His wife and children
greet him with affection despite the darkness
pawing the city streets. Laughing,
he searches his pockets for some peace offering:
a small mirror, silvered, gilted in bronze.
His children's faces radiate with wonder
to see themselves in the mirror's anteroom.
The body staring out from within.

ii. *Stormy Weather*

The woman sits combing her hair
in the oval-faced mirror,

her back turned to the young man
in the doorway; his wanting

so much to escape this lethargy
of sensation, this desire —

he wants to turn the mirror to the wall
the way some cultures do

to ward off lightning.
Bad weather.

What is moving beyond us,
ready to strike.

iii. *Bay Street*

All the bankers and young executives,
corporate lackeys, primp
expensive oxford shirts, paw at
unmussed hair in the polished
gleam of elevator doors

and I am reminded of Socrates,
how he urged his pupils to stare
into mirrors, into that nothingness,
urging them not to destroy,

through dishonourable thoughts or deeds,
whatever beauty they cannot see.

iv. Fun House

How to breathe in
an airless place

      this maze of glass

How did we come to see ourselves
as outside of the mirror

Bodies and minds
grown more abundant
upon reflection

      our flesh unfleshed

Wordlessly, we
stare into its absence
and suffer its look

v. Reflecting Stones

A mirror gathers more light than the human retina
but what does it see, alone in its own image,
ignored like a sulking child, seen not heard.
And what stories would it tell if given a chance
to move beyond sight and speak for itself?
You ask a question and it stares dumbly
from its corner of the room. A mirror looks
deeply into us the way we look deeply
into a stone polished by millennia of whitewater
or whispering sands to a speckless sheen.
Who is looking at who? The stones will not say.

vi. Mirror Images

A mirror is a sky of hoarfrost.
An arctic plain we will never walk upon.
An orchard of missing details.

A mirror is a clock that tells the body's time.
A wish formed in the mouth of a volcano.
An ice pond wrinkles skate across.

A mirror is a river of languid mercury.
The ghost of ourselves recognized
In doorways and storefronts

Passing between worlds of light and dark.
The invisible pared to the visible.
Everything we do not see and what that reflects.

WHAT'S LEFT TO WONDER ABOUT

TV is chewing gum for the eyes.

Frank Lloyd Wright

There is a part of me that understands why people centuries
      ago explored mysticism,
life as mystery. I am fascinated by those documentaries on
      cable TV

about crop circles or alien UFOs, mysterious tribes vanishing
      into Brazilian rainforests
never to be seen again. I'll sit for hours watching any program
      about Bigfoot,

or his Nepalese cousin, the Yeti, and imagine them both
      trekking through
old hardwood forest or wide Himalayan passes. I like to
      believe a chunk of wood

some man fried in teriyaki sauce really is a piece of Noah's
      Ark, that
Ogopogo and the Loch Ness Monster really are living
      descendants of dinosaurs.

I want for aliens to appear and for the past to be made to
      explain, once and for all,
how the pyramids were built. I want to touch something akin
      to wonder,

to rub a stone talisman, and feel its earth magic emanating up
      from within it.
I want to believe there are red-grottoed canals somewhere
      on Mars,

the last vestiges of a civilization which crumbled eons ago,
      but mostly
I want to live every day of my life in the embrace of mysteries
      that contain

so much of the blue frail endlessness that lies outside of
      myself:
there is nothing to do but hold onto them, until, one by one—
      they recant

and start pointing fingers at each other as the planet spins
      a little more
slowly on its axis for it, and the Man in the Moon
      sheds a few last tears.

We Have Ruins

We have ruins in this country,
not so old as Roman aqueducts
spilling up and down Italian countryside,
but we have ruins, homesteads and modest farms,
overgrown with bric-a-brac, usually
on the outskirts of town, places for kids
to dirt-bike through and find what treasures
time preserved: a blue bottle, bits of
rusted tins, a family of blackbirds living
in a crumbling fireplace, the timber-rot
of a pantry. Our ruins are just ruins.
Nothing to reassemble or reclaim.
The ruins in this country are forgotten,
like the people whose lives
gave out beneath them.

SMOKE

Looking through the smoke of years,
you see only fragments: a silver moon
marqueed against a small lake in early summer.
Tub-thumping insects floating out of dusk
to spark against cottage bug-zappers.
Little meteors. Shooting stars. It hardly matters.
There is still enough light to wish by.
And you see yourself, as a child, beside a campfire,
watching the last of the deadfall turn to ash
and thick-cloying smoke, tears burning your cheeks.
Sitting now, alone, by a dying fire,
you remember that night and how it felt.
You remember that sting of seeing.

DESIRE

Desire is an affliction of sense:
a breath inside a breath, flame
and flame's charred remains.
It is the pulse and purr
of the body's circuit:
a river of blue adrenaline
running through the brain's
thousand hungers.

Think of the West Indians,
how they put fireflies in cages,
or stuck them with gum to big toes
to light sundry paths through night,
cautious in avoiding snakes.

Desire is such darkness and flicker,
the unforseen leaping out,
a shape cold and reptilian
in the wind's mouthless night
waiting for something warm
to sink its teeth into.

Sonar

Bats surf and swing like sonic boomerangs
on the outskirts of town,

over low running hills, hunting the moths
of coming dusk. Night's shadow

cuts a ribbon of negative light across the fields,
telling me the sky and suburbs are a lie;

that everything we move into is outer space,
that everything has its opposite: the bat's echo

and the nothingness it encodes
speaks of life's animism and animateness.

Imagine white flames of moths slipstreaming above me—
their deaths bursting all over these hills.

The boy died: he left at dusk
with the last butterflies of summer.
A young man now sleeps in the gilded cage
of his bones. In his dream,
the boy returns—an old man
carrying his poverty and his shoes.
And moving very slowly, like one
who has lived a long time,
he pulls his shadow across the fields,
the moon's last remains.

ACKNOWLEDGEMENTS

I would like to thank the editors of *Carousel* and *The Antigonish Review* where some of my poems were first published. Many poems also appeared in a limited-run chapbook called *Form Letters* (Junction Books 2002).

§

There are a number of thank yous owing to a great many people, but I would be remiss if I didn't thank my family first: my parents, Gary and Bobbi, and my brother Derek and his family, Sarah and Coleson.

Thank yous also go out to the Concordia Writing program, especially to Sina Queyras and Shaun Leggett for long talks about poetry over many pints at the Stanley Pub.

My thanks to all my friends, old and new, who have contributed in their own way to my writing over the years: Cassandra Beach, Paul McNamara, Mary Harris, Gordon Marsden, J.R. (Tim) Struthers, Marianne Micros, John Huff, Mary di Michele, Gary Geddes, Robert Hilles, David Clink, John Stiles, Paul Vermeersch, Silas White, Carleton Wilson, and the staff and students at Bluevale Collegiate Institute.

PAUL MCNAMARA

ABOUT THE AUTHOR

Raised in the Ontario communities of Bancroft, Sioux Lookout and Stayner, where his father served postings as a small-town police officer, Chris Banks took his BA at the University of Guelph, a Master's in Creative Writing at Concordia and an education degree at Western. He currently works as an English and Creative Writing instructor at Bluevale Collegiate Institute in Waterloo, Ontario. His poetry has previously appeared in *Carousel* and *The Antigonish Review.*

A Junction Book

Typeset in TEFF Collis

TEFF Collis was designed in 1993 by Christoph Noordzij for The
Enschedé Font Foundry.

Printed and bound in Canada

EDITOR
Silas White

EDITOR FOR THE PRESS
Carleton Wilson

TYPESETTING
Carleton Wilson

COVER PHOTOGRAPH & DESIGN
Tim Franz

Junction Books
568 Indian Grove · Toronto, ON · M6P 2J4
www.junctionbooks.com

Nightwood Editions
www.nightwoodeditions.com